ESSENTIAL
Cakes

p

Contents

Introduction 4

Olive Oil, Fruit & Nut Cake 6

Chocolate & Pear Sponge 8

Clementine Cake .10

White Chocolate & Apricot Squares 12

Chocolate & Almond Torte 14

Carrot Cake 16

Lemon Syrup Cake 18

Apple Cake with Cider 20

Almond Cake 22

Apple Shortcakes .24

Cherry Scones 26

Cranberry Muffins 28

Sticky Chocolate Pudding 30

Fruit Crumble Tart 32

Lemon Tart 34

Coconut Cream Tart 36

Pine Kernel (Nut) Tart 38

Apricot & Cranberry Frangipane Tart 40

Crème Brûlée Tarts 42

Cinnamon & Sunflower Squares 44

Gingernuts 46

Caraway Biscuits (Cookies) 48

Peanut Butter Cookies 50

Hazelnut Squares .52

Coconut Flapjacks 54

Oat & Raisin Biscuits (Cookies) 56

Citrus Crescents .58

Lemon Jumbles 60

Chocolate & Lemon Pinwheels 62

White Chocolate Cookies 64

Shortbread Fantails 66

Millionaire's Shortbread 68

Vanilla Hearts 70

Rock Drops 72

Chocolate Chip Brownies 74

Chocolate Macaroons 76

Florentines 78

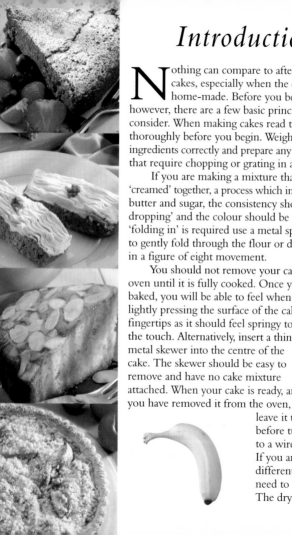

Introduction

Nothing can compare to afternoon tea and cakes, especially when the cakes are home-made. Before you begin baking however, there are a few basic principles to consider. When making cakes read the recipe thoroughly before you begin. Weigh all the ingredients correctly and prepare any ingredients that require chopping or grating in advance.

If you are making a mixture that has to be 'creamed' together, a process which involves creaming butter and sugar, the consistency should be 'soft dropping' and the colour should be almost white. If 'folding in' is required use a metal spoon or spatula to gently fold through the flour or dry ingredients in a figure of eight movement.

You should not remove your cake from the oven until it is fully cooked. Once your cake is baked, you will be able to feel when it is ready by lightly pressing the surface of the cake with your fingertips as it should feel springy to the touch. Alternatively, insert a thin metal skewer into the centre of the cake. The skewer should be easy to remove and have no cake mixture attached. When your cake is ready, and you have removed it from the oven,

leave it to cool in its tin before turning out on to a wire rack.

If you are making a tart different instructions need to be followed. The dry ingredients should be sieved into a large mixing bowl, then the diced fat should be added and tossed through the flour. By gently rubbing the fat between your fingertips a little at a time you should achieve a mixture of fine breadcrumbs. Whilst rubbing, aerate the mixture by lifting your hands up and dropping the mixture back into the bowl. Next, some iced water should be added to bind the mixture into a soft dough. The dough should be wrapped and put in to the fridge to chill for at least 30 minutes to make a successful tart.

Another favourite to be served with afternoon tea is the biscuit which is a sweet or savoury flat cake. The name biscuit actually derives from the French *bis* = twice + *cuit* = cooked. Therefore in theory the biscuit should be cooked twice, however this cooking method is generally no longer

required. To make delicious biscuits all you need are good ingredients. If using nuts they should be as fresh as possible, chocolate should be of excellent quality, an unrefined pure cane sugar should be used and as you will discover the best biscuits are made with butter. Biscuits should be left to cool on a wire rack once they are baked and like all cakes should be stored in an airtight container to maintain freshness.

Olive Oil, Fruit & Nut Cake

Serves 8

INGREDIENTS

225 g/8 oz/2 cups self-raising flour	125 ml/4 fl oz/$^{1}/_{2}$ cup milk	100 g/3$^{1}/_{2}$ oz mixed dried fruit
50 g/1$^{3}/_{4}$ oz/9 tsp caster (superfine) sugar	4 tbsp orange juice	25 g/1 oz pine kernels (nuts)
	150 ml/$^{1}/_{4}$ pint/$^{2}/_{3}$ cup olive oil	

1 Grease an 18 cm/7 inch cake tin (pan) and line with baking parchment.

2 Sieve (strain) the flour into a bowl and stir in the caster (superfine) sugar.

3 Make a well in the centre of the dry ingredients and pour in the milk and orange juice. Stir the mixture with a wooden spoon, beating in the flour and sugar.

4 Pour in the olive oil, stirring well so that all of the ingredients are evenly mixed.

5 Stir the mixed dried fruit and pine kernels (nuts) into the mixture and spoon into the prepared tin (pan).

6 Bake in a preheated oven, 180°C/350°F/Gas Mark 4, for about 45 minutes until the cake is golden and firm to the touch.

7 Leave the cake to cool in the tin (pan) for a few minutes, then transfer to a wire rack to cool.

8 Serve the cake warm or cold and cut into slices.

COOK'S TIP

Pine kernels (nuts) are best known as the flavouring ingredient in the classic Italian pesto, but here they give a delicate, slightly resinous flavour to this cake.

Chocolate & Pear Sponge

Serves 6

INGREDIENTS

175 g/6 oz/³/4 cup butter, softened	150 g/5¹/2 oz/1¹/4 cups self-raising flour	2 tbsp milk
175 g/6 oz/1 cup soft brown sugar	15 g/¹/2 oz/2 tbsp cocoa powder	2 small pears, peeled, cored and sliced
3 eggs, beaten		

1 Grease a 23 cm/8 inch loose-bottomed cake tin (pan) and line the base with baking parchment.

2 In a bowl, cream together the butter and soft brown sugar until pale and fluffy.

3 Gradually add the beaten eggs to the creamed mixture, beating well after each addition.

4 Sieve (strain) the self-raising flour and cocoa powder into the creamed mixture and fold in gently until all of the ingredients are combined.

5 Stir in the milk, then spoon the mixture into the prepared tin (pan). Level the surface with the back of a spoon or a knife.

6 Arrange the pear slices on top of the cake mixture, arranging them in a radiating pattern.

7 Bake in a preheated oven, 180°C/350°F/Gas Mark 4, for about 1 hour until the cake is just firm to the touch.

8 Leave the cake to cool in the tin (pan), then transfer to a wire rack until completely cold before serving.

COOK'S TIP

Serve the cake with melted chocolate drizzled over the top for a delicious dessert.

Clementine Cake

Serves 8

INGREDIENTS

2 clementines
175 g/6 oz/³/4 cup butter,
  softened
175 g/6 oz/³/4 cup caster
  (superfine) sugar

3 eggs, beaten
175 g/6 oz/1¹/2 cups self-
  raising flour
3 tbsp ground almonds
3 tbsp single (light) cream

GLAZE AND TOPPING:
6 tbsp clementine juice
2 tbsp caster (superfine) sugar
3 white sugar cubes, crushed

1 Grease an 18 cm/7 inch round tin (pan) and line the base with baking parchment.

2 Pare the rind from the clementines and chop the rind finely. In a bowl, cream together the butter, sugar and clementine rind until pale and fluffy.

3 Gradually add the beaten eggs to the mixture, beating well after each addition.

4 Gently fold in the self-raising flour followed by the ground almonds and the single (light) cream. Spoon the mixture into the prepared tin (pan).

5 Bake in a preheated oven, 180°C/350°F/ Gas Mark 4, for about 55-60 minutes or until a fine skewer inserted into the centre comes out clean. Leave to cool slightly.

6 To make the glaze, put the clementine juice into a small saucepan with the caster (superfine) sugar. Bring to the boil and simmer for 5 minutes.

7 Drizzle the glaze over the cake until it has been absorbed and sprinkle with the crushed sugar cubes.

COOK'S TIP

If you prefer, chop the rind from the clementines in a food processor or blender together with the sugar in step 2. Tip the mixture into a bowl with the butter and begin to cream the mixture.

White Chocolate & Apricot Squares

Makes 12 bars

INGREDIENTS

125 g/4^1/$_2$ oz/^{1}/$_2$ cup butter
175 g/6 oz white chocolate, chopped
4 eggs

125 g/4^1/$_2$ oz/^{1}/$_2$ cup caster (superfine) sugar
200 g/7 oz/1^3/$_4$ cups plain (all-purpose) flour, sieved (strained)

1 tsp baking powder
pinch of salt
100 g/3^1/$_2$ oz ready-to-eat dried apricots, chopped

1 Lightly grease a 20 cm/ 9 inch square cake tin (pan) and line the base with baking parchment.

2 Melt the butter and chocolate in a heatproof bowl set over a saucepan of simmering water. Stir frequently with a wooden spoon until the mixture is smooth and glossy. Remove from the heat and leave the mixture to cool slightly.

3 Beat the eggs and caster (superfine) sugar into the butter and chocolate mixture until well combined.

4 Fold in the flour, baking powder, salt and chopped dried apricots and mix well.

5 Pour the mixture into the tin (pan) and bake in a preheated oven, 180°C/350°F/Gas Mark 4, for 25–30 minutes.

6 The centre of the cake may not be completely firm, but it will set as it cools. Leave in the tin (pan) to cool.

7 When the cake is completely cold turn it out and slice into bars or squares.

VARIATION

Replace the white chocolate with milk or dark chocolate, if you prefer.

Chocolate & Almond Torte

Serves 10

INGREDIENTS

225 g/8 oz dark chocolate, broken into pieces
3 tbsp water
150 g/5^1/$_2$ oz/1 cup soft brown sugar
175 g/6 oz/^{3}/$_4$ cup butter, softened

25 g/1 oz/^{1}/$_4$ cup ground almonds
3 tbsp self-raising flour
5 eggs, separated
100 g 3^1/$_2$ oz/^{1}/$_4$ cup blanched almonds, chopped finely

icing (confectioners') sugar, for dusting
double (heavy) cream, to serve (optional)

1 Grease a 23 cm/9 inch loose-bottomed cake tin (pan) and base line with baking parchment.

2 In a saucepan set over a very low heat, melt the chocolate with the water, stirring until smooth. Add the sugar and stir until dissolved, taking the pan off the heat to prevent it overheating.

3 Add the butter in small amounts until it has melted into the chocolate.

Remove from the heat and lightly stir in the ground almonds and flour. Add the egg yolks one at a time, beating well after each addition.

4 In a large mixing bowl, whisk the egg whites until they stand in soft peaks, then fold them into the chocolate mixture with a metal spoon. Stir in the chopped almonds. Pour the mixture into the tin (pan) and level the surface with a palette knife (spatula).

5 Bake in a preheated oven, 180°C/350°F/ Gas Mark 4, for about 40-45 minutes until well risen and firm (the cake will crack on the surface during cooking).

6 Leave the cake to cool in the tin (pan) for 30-40 minutes, then turn it out on to a wire rack to cool completely. Dust with icing (confectioners') sugar and serve in slices with double (heavy) cream, if using.

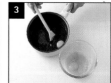

Carrot Cake

Makes 12 bars

INGREDIENTS

125 g/4^1/2 oz/1 cup self-
    raising flour
pinch of salt
1 tsp ground cinnamon
125 g/4^1/2 oz/^{3}/4 cup soft
    brown sugar
2 eggs
100 ml/3^1/2 fl oz/scant ^{1}/2 cup
    sunflower oil

125 g/4^1/2 oz carrot, peeled
    and grated finely
25 g/1 oz/^{1}/3 cup desiccated
    (shredded) coconut
25 g/1 oz/^{1}/3 cup walnuts,
    chopped
walnut pieces, for decoration

FROSTING:
50 g/1^3/4 oz/10 tsp butter,
    softened
50 g/1^3/4 oz full fat soft
    cheese
225 g/8 oz/1^1/2 cups icing
    (confectioners') sugar,
    sieved (strained)
1 tsp lemon juice

1 Lightly grease a
20 cm/8 inch square
cake tin (pan) and line with
baking parchment.

2 Sieve (strain) the flour,
salt and ground
cinnamon into a large bowl
and stir in the brown sugar.
Add the eggs and oil to
the dry ingredients and
mix well.

3 Stir in the grated
carrot, desiccated

(shredded) coconut and
chopped walnuts.

4 Pour the mixture into
the prepared tin (pan)
and bake in a preheated
oven, 180°C/350°F/Gas
Mark 4, for 20-25 minutes
or until just firm to the
touch. Leave to cool in the
tin (pan).

5 Meanwhile, make the
cheese frosting. In a
bowl, beat together the

butter, full fat soft cheese,
icing (confectioners')
sugar and lemon juice
until the mixture is fluffy
and creamy.

6 Turn the cake out of
the tin (pan) and cut
into 12 bars or slices.
Spread with the frosting
and then decorate with
walnut pieces.

Lemon Syrup Cake

Serves 8

INGREDIENTS

200 g/7 oz/1¾ cups plain (all-purpose) flour
2 tsp baking powder
200 g/7 oz/1 cup caster (superfine) sugar
4 eggs

150 ml/¼ pint/⅔ cup soured cream
grated rind 1 large lemon
4 tbsp lemon juice
150 ml/¼ pint/⅔ cup sunflower oil

SYRUP:
4 tbsp icing (confectioners') sugar
3 tbsp lemon juice

1 Lightly grease a 20 cm/8 inch loose-bottomed round cake tin (pan) and line the base with baking parchment.

2 Sieve (strain) the flour and baking powder into a mixing bowl and stir in the sugar.

3 In a separate bowl, whisk the eggs, soured cream, lemon rind, lemon juice and oil together.

4 Pour the egg mixture into the dry ingredients and mix well until evenly combined.

5 Pour the mixture into the prepared tin (pan) and bake in a preheated oven, 180°C 350°F/Gas Mark 4, for 45–60 minutes until risen and golden brown.

6 To make the syrup, mix together the icing (confectioners') sugar and lemon juice in a small saucepan. Stir over a low heat until just beginning to bubble and turn syrupy.

7 As soon as the cake comes out of the oven prick the surface with a fine skewer, then brush the syrup over the top. Leave the cake to cool completely in the tin (pan) before turning out and serving.

COOK'S TIP

Pricking the surface of the hot cake with a skewer ensures that the syrup seeps right into the cake.

Apple Cake with Cider

Makes a 20 cm/8 inch cake

INGREDIENTS

225 g/8 oz/2 cups self-raising
flour
1 tsp baking powder
75 g/2³/4 oz/¹/3 cup butter,
cut into small pieces
75 g/2³/4 oz/¹/3 cup caster
(superfine) sugar

50 g/1³/4 oz dried apple,
chopped
75 g/2³/4 oz/5 tbsp raisins
150 ml/¹/4 pint/²/3 cup sweet
cider

1 egg, beaten
175 g/6 oz raspberries

1 Grease a 20 cm/8 inch cake tin (pan) and line with baking parchment.

2 Sieve (strain) the flour and baking powder into a mixing bowl and rub in the butter with your fingers until the mixture resembles fine breadcrumbs.

3 Stir in the caster (superfine) sugar, chopped dried apple and raisins, and mix well.

4 Pour in the sweet cider and egg and mix together until thoroughly blended. Stir in the raspberries very gently so they do not break up.

5 Pour the mixture into the prepared cake tin (pan).

6 Bake in a preheated oven, 190°C/375°F/ Gas Mark 5, for about 40 minutes until risen and lightly golden. Leave the cake to cool in the tin

(pan), then turn out on to a wire rack. Leave until completely cold before serving.

VARIATION

If you don't want to use cider, replace it with clear apple juice, if you prefer.

Almond Cake

Serves 8

INGREDIENTS

100 g/3¹/₂ oz/¹/₃ cup soft tub margarine
50 g/1³/₄ oz/3 tbsp soft brown sugar
2 eggs
175 g/6 oz/1¹/₂ cups self-raising flour

1 tsp baking powder
4 tbsp milk
2 tbsp runny honey
50 g/1³/₄ oz/¹/₂ cup flaked almonds

SYRUP:
150 ml/¹/₄ pint/²/₃ cup runny honey
2 tbsp lemon juice

1 Grease an 18 cm/7 inch round cake tin (pan) and line with baking parchment.

2 Place the margarine, brown sugar, eggs, flour, baking powder, milk and honey in a large mixing bowl and beat well for about 1 minute until all of the ingredients are thoroughly mixed together.

3 Spoon into the prepared tin (pan), level the surface with the back of a spoon or a knife and sprinkle with the almonds.

4 Bake in a preheated oven, 180°C/350°F/ Gas Mark 4, for about 50 minutes or until the cake is well risen.

5 Meanwhile, make the syrup. Combine the honey and lemon juice in a small saucepan and simmer for about 5 minutes or until the syrup starts to coat the back of a spoon.

6 As soon as the cake comes out of the oven, pour over the syrup, allowing it to seep into the middle of the cake.

7 Leave the cake to cool for at least 2 hours before slicing.

Apple Shortcakes

Makes 4

INGREDIENTS

---

150 g/5^1/$_2$ oz/1^1/$_4$ cups plain (all-purpose) flour
^{1}/$_2$ tsp salt
1 tsp baking powder
1 tbsp caster (superfine) sugar
25 g/1 oz/6 tsp butter, cut into small pieces
50 ml/2 fl oz/^{1}/$_4$ cup milk

icing (confectioners') sugar, for dusting

FILLING:
3 dessert apples, peeled, cored and sliced
100 g/3^1/$_2$ oz/^{1}/$_2$ cup caster (superfine) sugar

1 tbsp lemon juice
1 tsp ground cinnamon
300 ml/^{1}/$_2$ pint/1^1/$_3$ cups water
150 ml/^{1}/$_4$ pint/^{2}/$_3$ cup double (heavy) cream, whipped lightly

---

1 Lightly grease a baking tray (cookie sheet).

2 Sieve (strain) the flour, salt and baking powder into a bowl. Stir in the sugar, then rub in the butter until the mixture resembles fine breadcrumbs. Pour in the milk and mix everything to a soft dough.

3 Knead the dough, then roll out to a thickness of 1 cm/^{1}/$_2$ inch. Stamp out 4 rounds, using a 5 cm/2 inch cutter. Transfer the rounds to the prepared baking tray (sheet). Bake in a preheated oven, 220°C/425°F/Gas Mark 7, for about 15 minutes until the shortcakes are well risen and lightly browned. Leave to cool.

4 To make the filling, place the apple slices, sugar, lemon juice and cinnamon in a saucepan. Add the water, bring to the boil and simmer uncovered for 5-10 minutes until the apples are tender. Leave to cool a little, then remove the apples from the pan.

5 To serve, split the shortcakes in half. Place each bottom half on an individual serving plate and spoon on a quarter of the apple slices, then the cream. Place the other half of the shortcake on top. Serve dusted with icing (confectioners') sugar, if wished.

Cherry Scones

Makes 8

INGREDIENTS

225 g/8 oz/2 cups self-raising flour	75 g/2³/4 oz/¹/3 cup butter, cut into small pieces	40 g/1¹/2 oz/3 tbsp sultanas (golden raisins)
1 tbsp caster (superfine) sugar	40 g/1¹/2 oz/3 tbsp glacé (candied) cherries, chopped	1 egg, beaten
pinch of salt		50 ml/2 fl oz/¹/4 cup milk

1 Lightly grease a baking tray (cookie sheet).

2 Sieve (strain) the flour, sugar and salt into a mixing bowl and rub in the butter with your fingers until the scone mixture resembles breadcrumbs.

3 Stir in the glacé (candied) cherries and sultanas (golden raisins). Add the beaten egg.

4 Reserve 1 tablespoon of the milk for glazing, then add the remainder to the mixture. Mix together to form a soft dough.

5 On a floured surface, roll out the dough to a thickness of 2 cm/³/4 inches and cut out 8 scones, using a 5 cm/2 inch cutter.

6 Place the scones on to the baking tray (cookie sheet) and brush with the reserved milk.

7 Bake in a preheated oven, 220°C/425°F/Gas Mark 7, for 8-10 minutes or until the scones are golden brown.

8 Leave to cool on a wire rack, then serve split and buttered.

COOK'S TIP

These scones will freeze very successfully but they are best defrosted and eaten within 1 month.

Cranberry Muffins

Makes 18

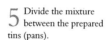

INGREDIENTS

225 g/8 oz/2 cups plain (all-purpose) flour
2 tsp baking powder
1/2 tsp salt

50 g/1³/4 oz/9 tsp caster (superfine) sugar
50 g/1³/4 oz/10 tsp butter, melted
2 eggs, beaten

200 ml/7 fl oz/³/4 cup milk
100 g/3¹/2 oz fresh cranberries
2 tbsp freshly grated Parmesan cheese

1 Lightly grease 2 bun (patty) tins (pans).

2 Sieve (strain) the flour, baking powder and salt into a mixing bowl. Stir in the caster (superfine) sugar.

3 In a separate bowl, mix the butter, beaten eggs and milk together, then pour into the bowl of dry ingredients.

4 Mix lightly together until all of the ingredients are evenly combined, then stir in the fresh cranberries.

5 Divide the mixture between the prepared tins (pans).

6 Sprinkle the grated Parmesan cheese over the top of each muffin mixture.

7 Bake in a preheated oven, 200°C/400°F/Gas Mark 6, for about 20 minutes or until the muffins are well risen and a golden brown colour.

8 Leave the muffins to cool in the tins (pans). Transfer the muffins to a wire rack and leave to cool completely before serving.

VARIATION

For a sweet alternative to this recipe, replace the Parmesan cheese with demerara (brown crystal) sugar in step 6, if you prefer.

Sticky Chocolate Pudding

Serves 6

INGREDIENTS

125 g/4½ oz/½ cup butter,
  softened
150 g/5½ oz/¾ cup soft
  brown sugar
3 eggs, beaten
pinch of salt
25 g/1 oz cocoa powder

125 g/4½ oz/1 cup self-
  raising flour
25 g/1 oz dark chocolate,
  chopped finely
75 g/2¾ oz white chocolate,
  chopped finely

SAUCE:
150 ml/5 fl oz/⅔ cup double
  (heavy) cream
75 g/2¾ oz/⅓ cup soft
  brown sugar
25 g/1 oz/6 tsp butter

1 Lightly grease 6 individual 175 ml/6 fl oz/¾ cup pudding basins (molds).

2 Cream together the butter and sugar until pale and fluffy. Beat in the eggs a little at a time.

3 Sieve (strain) the salt, cocoa powder and flour into the creamed mixture and fold through the mixture. Stir the chopped chocolate evenly into the mixture.

4 Divide the mixture between the prepared pudding basins (molds). Lightly grease 6 squares of foil and use them to cover the basins (molds). Press around the edges to seal.

5 Place the basins (molds) in a roasting tin (pan) and add boiling water to come halfway up the sides of the basins (molds).

6 Bake in a preheated oven, 180°/350°F/Gas Mark 4, for 50 minutes, or until a skewer inserted into the centre comes out clean. Remove the basins (molds) from the tin and set aside.

7 To make the sauce, put the cream, sugar and butter into a pan and bring to the boil over a gentle heat. Simmer gently until the sugar has dissolved.

8 Turn the puddings out on to serving plates, pour the sauce over the top and serve immediately.

Fruit Crumble Tart

Serves 8

INGREDIENTS

PASTRY (PIE DOUGH):
150 g/5 oz/1$\frac{1}{4}$ cups plain (all-purpose) flour
25 g/1 oz/5 tsp caster (superfine) sugar
125 g/4$\frac{1}{2}$ oz/$\frac{1}{2}$ cup butter, cut into small pieces
1 tbsp water

FILLING:
250 g/9 oz raspberries
450 g/1 lb plums, halved, stoned and chopped roughly
3 tbsp demerara (brown crystal) sugar

TO SERVE:
single (light) cream

TOPPING:
125 g/4$\frac{1}{2}$ oz/1 cup plain (all-purpose) flour
75 g/2$\frac{3}{4}$ oz/$\frac{1}{3}$ cup demerara (brown crystal) sugar
100 g/3$\frac{1}{2}$ oz/$\frac{1}{3}$ cup butter, cut into small pieces
100 g/3$\frac{1}{2}$ oz chopped mixed nuts
1 tsp ground cinnamon

1 To make the pastry (pie dough), place the flour, sugar and butter in a bowl and rub in the butter with your fingers. Add the water and work the mixture together until a soft pastry (pie dough) has formed. Wrap and leave to chill for 30 minutes.

2 Roll out the pastry (pie dough) to line the base of a 24 cm/9$\frac{1}{2}$ inch loose-bottomed quiche/flan tin (pan). Prick the base of the pastry (pie dough) with a fork and leave to chill for about 30 minutes.

3 To make the filling, toss the raspberries and plums together with the sugar and spoon into the pastry case (pie shell).

4 To make the crumble topping, combine the flour, sugar and butter. Work the butter into the flour with your fingers until the mixture resembles coarse breadcrumbs. Stir in the nuts and cinnamon.

5 Sprinkle the topping over the fruit and bake in a preheated oven, 200°C/400°F/Gas Mark 6, for 20-25 minutes until golden. Serve the tart with single (light) cream.

Lemon Tart

Serves 8

INGREDIENTS

PASTRY (PIE DOUGH):
150 g/5^1/2 oz/1^1/4 cups plain
    (all-purpose) flour
25 g/1 oz/5 tsp caster
    (superfine) sugar
125 g/4^1/2 oz/^{1}/2 cup butter,
    cut into small pieces

1 tbsp water

FILLING:
150 ml/^{1}/4 pint/^{2}/3 cup
    double (heavy) cream
100 g/3^1/2 oz/^{1}/2 cup caster
    (superfine) sugar

4 eggs
grated rind of 3 lemons
12 tbsp lemon juice
icing (confectioners') sugar,
    for dusting

1 To make the pastry (pie dough), place the flour and sugar in a bowl and rub in the butter. Add the water and mix until a soft pastry (pie dough) has formed. Wrap and leave to chill for 30 minutes.

2 On a lightly floured surface, roll out the dough and line a 24 cm/ 9½ inch loose-bottomed quiche/flan tin (pan). Prick the pastry (pie dough) with a fork and leave to chill for 30 minutes.

3 Line the pastry case (pie shell) with foil and baking beans and bake in a preheated oven, 190°C/ 375°F/ Gas Mark 5, for 15 minutes. Remove the foil and beans and cook for a further 15 minutes.

4 To make the filling, whisk the cream, sugar, eggs, lemon rind and juice together. Place the pastry case (pie shell), still in its tin (pan), on a baking tray (cookie sheet) and pour in the filling.

5 Bake in the oven for about 20 minutes or until just set. Leave to cool, then lightly dust with icing (confectioners') sugar before serving.

Coconut Cream Tart

Serves 6-8

INGREDIENTS

PASTRY (PIE DOUGH):
150 g/5^1/2 oz/1^1/4 cups plain
(all-purpose) flour
25 g/1 oz/5 tsp caster
(superfine) sugar
125 g/4^1/2 oz/^{1}/2 cup butter,
cut into small pieces
1 tbsp water

FILLING:
425 ml/^{3}/4 pint/2 cups milk
125 g /4^1/2 oz creamed
coconut
3 egg yolks
125 g/4^1/2 oz/^{1}/2 cup caster
(superfine) sugar
50 g/1^3/4 oz/^{1}/2 cup plain (all-
purpose) flour, sieved

25 g/1 oz/^{1}/3 cup desiccated
(shredded) coconut
25 g/1 oz glacé (candied)
pineapple, chopped, plus
extra to decorate
2 tbsp rum or pineapple juice
300 ml/^{1}/2 pint/1^1/3 cups
whipping cream, whipped,
plus extra to decorate

1 Place the flour and sugar in a bowl and rub in the butter. Add the water and work the mixture together until a soft pastry (pie dough) has formed. Wrap and leave to chill for 30 minutes.

2 Roll out the dough and line a 24 cm/9½ inch loose-bottomed quiche/flan tin (pan). Prick the pastry with a fork and leave to chill for 30 minutes. Line the pastry case (pie shell) with foil and baking beans and bake in a preheated oven, 190°C/375°F/Gas 5, for 15 minutes. Remove the foil and beans and cook for a further 15 minutes. Leave to cool.

3 To make the filling, bring the milk and creamed coconut to just below boiling point, stirring to melt the coconut.

4 Whisk the egg yolks with the sugar until fluffy. Whisk in the flour. Add the hot milk, stirring. Return the mixture to the pan and gently heat for 8 minutes until thick, stirring. Leave to cool.

5 Stir in the coconut, pineapple and rum and spread the filling in the pastry case (pie shell). Cover with the whipped cream, decorate and chill.

Pine Kernel (Nut) Tart

Serves 8

INGREDIENTS

PASTRY (PIE DOUGH):
150 g /5 oz/1^1/4 cups plain
  (all-purpose) flour
25 g/1 oz/5 tsp caster
  (superfine) sugar
125 g/4^1/2 oz/^{1}/2 cup butter,
  cut into small pieces

1 tbsp water

FILLING:
350 g/12 oz curd cheese
4 tbsp double (heavy) cream
3 eggs

125 g/4^1/2 oz/^{1}/2 cup caster
  (superfine) sugar
grated rind of 1 orange
100 g/3^1/2 oz pine kernels
  (nuts)

1 To make the pastry (pie dough), place the flour and sugar in a bowl and rub in the butter with your fingers. Add the water and work the mixture together until a soft pastry (pie dough) has formed. Wrap and leave to chill for 30 minutes.

2 On a lightly floured surface, roll out the dough and line a 24 cm/ 9½ inch loose-bottomed quiche/flan tin (pan). Prick the pastry (pie dough) with a fork and leave to chill for 30 minutes.

3 Line the pastry case (pie shell) with foil and baking beans and bake in a preheated oven, 190°C/ 375°F/ Gas Mark 5, for 15 minutes. Remove the foil and beans and cook the pastry case (pie shell) for a further 15 minutes.

4 To make the filling, beat together the curd cheese, cream, eggs, sugar, orange rind and half of the pine kernels (nuts). Pour the filling into the pastry case (pie shell) and sprinkle over the remaining pine kernels (nuts).

5 Bake in the oven at 170°C/325°F/Gas Mark 3 for 35 minutes or until just set. Leave to cool before serving.

Apricot & Cranberry Frangipane Tart

Serves 8–10

INGREDIENTS

PASTRY (PIE DOUGH):
150 g/5$^1/_2$ oz/1$^1/_4$ cups plain
  (all-purpose) flour
125 g/4$^1/_2$ oz/$^1/_2$ cup caster
  (superfine) sugar
125 g/4$^1/_2$ oz/$^1/_2$ cup butter,
  cut into small pieces
1 tbsp water

FILLING:
200 g/7 oz/1 cup unsalted
  butter
200 g/7 oz/1 cup caster
  (superfine) sugar
1 egg
2 egg yolks
40 g/1$^1/_2$ oz/6 tbsp plain (all-
  purpose) flour, sieved
  (strained)

175 g/6 oz/1$^2/_3$ cups ground
  almonds
4 tbsp double (heavy) cream
411 g/14$^1/_2$ oz can apricot
  halves, drained
125 g/4$^1/_2$ oz fresh
  cranberries

1 Place the flour and sugar in a bowl and rub in the butter. Add the water and work the mixture together until a soft pastry (pie dough) has formed. Wrap and leave to chill for 30 minutes.

2 On a lightly floured surface, roll out the dough and line a 24 cm/9$^1/_2$ inch loose-bottomed quiche/flan tin (pan). Prick the pastry (pie dough) with a fork and chill for 30 minutes.

3 Line the pastry case (pie shell) with foil and baking beans and bake in a preheated oven, 190°C/375°F/Gas Mark 5, for 15 minutes. Remove the foil and beans and cook for a further 10 minutes.

4 Cream together the butter and sugar until fluffy. Beat in the egg and egg yolks, and stir in the flour, almonds and cream.

5 Place the apricots and cranberries in the pastry case (pie shell) and spoon the filling on top.

6 Bake in the oven for about 1 hour, or until the topping is just set. Leave to cool slightly, then serve warm or cold.

Crème Brûlée Tarts

Makes 6

INGREDIENTS

PASTRY (PIE DOUGH):
150 g/5 oz/1¹/₄ cups plain (all-
   purpose) flour
25 g/1 oz/5 tsp caster
   (superfine) sugar
125 g/4¹/₂ oz/¹/₂ cup butter,
   cut into small pieces.

1 tbsp water

FILLING:
4 egg yolks
50 g/ 1³/₄ oz/9 tsp caster
   (superfine) sugar

400 ml 14 fl oz/1³/₄ cups
   double (heavy) cream
1 tsp vanilla flavouring
   (extract)
demerara (brown crystal)
   sugar, for sprinkling

1 Place the flour and sugar in a bowl and rub in the butter. Add the water and work the mixture together until a soft pastry (pie dough) forms. Wrap and chill for 30 minutes.

2 Roll out the dough to line six 10 cm/4 inch tart tins (pans). Prick the bottom of the pastry (pie dough) with a fork and leave to chill for 20 minutes

3 Line the pastry cases (pie shells) with foil

and baking beans and bake in a preheated oven, 190°C/375°F/Gas Mark 5, for 15 minutes. Remove the foil and beans and cook for 10 minutes until crisp and golden. Leave to cool.

4 Beat the egg yolks and sugar until pale. Heat the cream and vanilla until just below boiling point, then add to the egg mixture, whisking constantly.

5 Place the mixture in a pan and bring to just

below the boil, stirring until thick. Do not allow to boil or it will curdle.

6 Leave the mixture to cool slightly, then pour it into the tart tins (pans). Leave to cool and then leave to chill overnight.

7 Sprinkle the tarts with the sugar. Place under a preheated hot grill (broiler) for a few minutes. Leave to cool, then chill for 2 hours before serving.

Cinnamon & Sunflower Squares

Makes 12

INGREDIENTS

250 g/9 oz/1 cup butter,
softened
250 g/9 oz/1¹/₄ cups caster
(superfine) sugar
3 eggs, beaten

250 g/9 oz/2 cups self-raising
flour
¹/₂ tsp bicarbonate of soda
(baking soda)

1 tbsp ground cinnamon
150 ml/¹/₄ pint/²/₃ cup
soured cream
100 g/3¹/₂ oz sunflower seeds

1 Grease a 23 cm/9 inch square cake tin (pan) and line the base with baking parchment.

2 In a large mixing bowl, cream together the butter and caster (superfine) sugar until the mixture is light and fluffy.

3 Gradually add the beaten eggs to the mixture, beating well after each addition.

4 Sieve (strain) the self-raising flour, bicarbonate of soda (baking soda) and ground cinnamon into the creamed mixture and fold in gently, using a metal spoon.

5 Spoon in the soured cream and sunflower seeds and gently mix until well combined.

6 Spoon the mixture into the prepared cake tin (pan) and level the surface with the back of a spoon or a knife.

7 Bake in a preheated oven, 180°C/350°F/Gas Mark 4, for 45 minutes until the mixture is firm to the touch when pressed with a finger.

8 Loosen the edges with a round-bladed knife, then turn out on to a wire rack to cool completely. Slice into 12 squares.

COOK'S TIP

*These moist squares
will freeze
well and will keep for up
to 1 month.*

Gingernuts

Makes 30

INGREDIENTS

350 g/12 oz/3 cups self-raising (self-rising) flour
pinch of salt
200 g/7 oz/1 cup caster (superfine) sugar

1 tbsp ground ginger
1 tsp bicarbonate of soda (baking soda)
125 g/4^1/2 oz/^{1}/2 cup butter

75 g/2^3/4 oz/^{1}/4 cup golden (light corn) syrup
1 egg, beaten
1 tsp grated orange rind

1 Lightly grease several baking trays (cookie sheets).

2 Sieve (strain) the flour, salt, sugar, ginger and bicarbonate of soda (baking soda) into a large mixing bowl.

3 Heat the butter and golden (light corn) syrup together in a saucepan over a very low heat until the butter has melted.

4 Leave the butter mixture to cool slightly, then pour it on to the dry ingredients.

5 Add the egg and orange rind and mix well.

6 Using your hands, carefully shape the dough into 30 even-sized balls.

7 Place the balls well apart on the prepared baking trays (cookie sheets), then flatten them slightly with your fingers.

8 Bake in a preheated oven, 160°C/325°F/ Gas Mark 3, for 15-20 minutes, then transfer them to a wire rack to cool.

VARIATION

If you like your gingernuts crunchy, bake them in the oven for a few minutes longer.

Caraway Biscuits (Cookies)

Makes about 36

> **INGREDIENTS**
>
> 225 g/8 oz/2 cups plain (all-purpose) flour
> pinch of salt
> 100 g/3½ oz/⅓ cup butter, cut into small pieces
>
> 225 g/8 oz/1¼ cups caster (superfine) sugar
> 1 egg, beaten
>
> 2 tbsp caraway seeds
> demerara (brown crystal) sugar, for sprinkling (optional)

1 Lightly grease several baking trays (cookie sheets).

2 Sieve (strain) the flour and salt into a mixing bowl. Rub in the butter with your fingers until the mixture resembles fine breadcrumbs. Stir in the caster (superfine) sugar.

3 Reserve 1 tbsp beaten egg for brushing the biscuits (cookies). Add the rest of the egg and the caraway seeds to the mixture and bring together to form a soft dough.

4 On a lightly floured surface, roll out the biscuit (cookie) dough thinly and then cut out about 36 rounds with a 6 cm/2½ inch biscuit (cookie) cutter.

5 Transfer the rounds to the prepared baking trays (cookie sheets), brush with the reserved egg and sprinkle with demerara (brown crystal) sugar.

6 Bake in a preheated oven, 160°C/325°F/ Gas 3, for 15 minutes until lightly golden and crisp.

7 Leave the biscuits (cookies) to cool on a wire rack and store in an airtight container.

VARIATION

Caraway seeds have a nutty, delicate anise flavour. If you don't like their flavour, replace the caraway seeds with the milder-flavoured poppy seeds.

Peanut Butter Cookies

Makes 20

INGREDIENTS

125 g/4^1/2 oz/^{1}/2 cup butter, softened
150 g/5^1/2 oz/^{1}/2 cup chunky peanut butter
225 g/8 oz/1 cup granulated sugar

1 egg, lightly beaten
150 g/5^1/2 oz/1^1/4 cup plain (all-purpose) flour
^{1}/2 tsp baking powder

pinch of salt
75 g/2 ^{3}/4 oz unsalted natural peanuts, chopped

1 Lightly grease 2 baking trays (cookie sheets).

2 In a large mixing bowl, beat together the butter and peanut butter.

3 Gradually add the sugar and beat well.

4 Add the beaten egg a little at a time until it is thoroughly combined.

5 Sieve (strain) the flour, baking powder and salt into the peanut butter mixture.

6 Add the peanuts and bring all of the ingredients together to form a soft dough. Wrap and leave to chill for about 30 minutes.

7 Form the dough into 20 balls and place them on to the prepared baking trays (cookie sheets) about 5 cm/2 inches apart to allow for spreading. Flatten them slightly with your hand.

8 Bake in a preheated oven, 190°C/375°F/ Gas Mark 5, for 15 minutes until golden brown. Transfer the biscuits (cookies) to a wire rack and leave to cool.

COOK'S TIP

For a crunchy bite and sparkling appearance, sprinkle the biscuits (cookies) with demerara (brown crystal) sugar before baking.

Hazelnut Squares

Makes 16

INGREDIENTS

150 g/5^1/$_2$ oz/1^1/$_4$ cups plain
  (all-purpose) flour
pinch of salt
1 tsp baking powder

100 g/3^1/$_2$ oz/^{1}/$_3$ cup butter,
  cut into small pieces
150 g/5^1/$_2$ oz/1 cup soft
  brown sugar
1 egg, beaten
4 tbsp milk

100 g/3^1/$_2$ oz/1 cup hazelnuts,
  halved
demerara (brown crystal)
  sugar, for sprinkling
  (optional)

1 Grease a 23 cm/9 inch square cake tin (pan) and line the base with baking parchment.

2 Sieve (strain) the flour, salt and baking powder into a large mixing bowl.

3 Rub in the butter with your fingers until the mixture resembles fine breadcrumbs. Stir in the brown sugar.

4 Add the egg, milk and nuts to the mixture and mix well.

5 Spoon the mixture into the prepared cake tin (pan) and level the surface. Sprinkle with demerara (brown crystal) sugar, if using.

6 Bake in a preheated oven, 180°C/350°F/Gas Mark 4, for about 25 minutes or until the mixture is firm to the touch when pressed with a finger.

7 Leave to cool for 10 minutes, then loosen the edges with a round-bladed knife and turn out on to a wire rack. Cut into squares.

VARIATION

For a coffee time biscuit (cookie), replace the milk with the same amount of cold strong black coffee, the stronger the better!

Coconut Flapjacks

Makes 16 squares

INGREDIENTS

200 g/7 oz/1 cup butter
200 g /7 oz/1¹/₃ cups
   demerara (brown crystal)
   sugar

2 tbsp golden (light corn)
   syrup
275 g/9¹/₂ oz/3¹/₂ cups
   porridge oats
100 g/3¹/₂ oz/1 cup desiccated
   (shredded) coconut

75 g/2³/₄ oz/¹/₃ cup glacé
   (candied) cherries, chopped

1 Lightly grease a 30 × 23 cm/12 × 9 inch baking tray (cookie sheet).

2 Heat the butter, demerara (brown crystal) sugar and golden (light corn) syrup in a large saucepan until just melted.

3 Stir in the oats, desiccated (shredded) coconut and glacé (candied) cherries and mix until evenly combined.

4 Spread the mixture on to the baking tray (cookie sheet) and press down with the back of a palette knife (spatula) to make a smooth surface.

5 Bake in a preheated oven, 170°C/325°F/ Gas Mark 3, for about 30 minutes.

6 Remove from the oven and leave to cool on the baking tray (cookie sheet) for 10 minutes.

7 Cut the mixture into squares using a sharp knife.

8 Carefully transfer the flapjacks to a wire rack and leave to cool completely.

COOK'S TIP

The flapjacks are best stored in an airtight container and eaten within 1 week. They can also be frozen for up to 1 month.

Oat & Raisin Biscuits (Cookies)

Makes 10

INGREDIENTS

50 g/1³/4 oz/10 tsp butter
125 g/4¹/2 oz/¹/2 cup caster (superfine) sugar
1 egg, beaten

50 g/1³/4 oz/¹/2 cup plain (all-purpose) flour
¹/2 tsp salt
¹/2 tsp baking powder

175 g/6 oz/2 cups porridge oats
125 g/4¹/2 oz/³/4 cup raisins
2 tbsp sesame seeds

1 Lightly grease 2 baking trays (cookie sheets).

2 In a large mixing bowl, cream together the butter and sugar until light and fluffy.

3 Add the beaten egg gradually and beat until well combined.

4 Sieve (strain) the flour, salt and baking powder into the creamed mixture. Mix well.

5 Add the porridge oats, raisins and sesame seeds and mix well.

6 Place spoonfuls of the mixture well apart on the prepared baking trays (cookie sheets) and flatten them slightly with the back of a spoon.

7 Bake in a preheated oven, 180°C/350°F/Gas Mark 4, for 15 minutes.

8 Leave the biscuits (cookies) to cool slightly on the baking trays (cookie sheets).

9 Transfer the biscuits (cookies) to a wire rack and leave to cool completely before serving.

VARIATION

Substitute chopped ready-to-eat dried apricots for the raisins, if you prefer.

COOK'S TIP

To enjoy these biscuits (cookies) at their best, store them in an airtight container.

Citrus Crescents

Makes about 25

INGREDIENTS

100 g/3¹/2 oz/¹/3 cup butter, softened
75 g/2³/4 oz/¹/3 cup caster (superfine) sugar
1 egg, separated

200 g/7 oz/1¹/4 cups plain (all-purpose) flour
grated rind of 1 orange
grated rind of 1 lemon

grated rind of 1 lime
2-3 tbsp orange juice
caster (superfine) sugar, for sprinkling (optional)

1 Lightly grease 2 baking trays (cookie sheets).

2 In a mixing bowl, cream together the butter and sugar until light and fluffy, then gradually beat in the egg yolk.

3 Sieve (strain) the flour into the creamed mixture and mix well. Add the orange, lemon and lime rinds with enough of the orange juice to make a soft dough.

4 Roll out the dough on a lightly floured surface. Stamp out rounds using a 7.5 cm/3 inch biscuit (cookie) cutter. Make crescent shapes out of the rounds by cutting away a quarter of each round. Re-roll the trimmings to make about 25 crescents.

5 Place the crescents on to the prepared baking trays (cookie sheets). Prick the surface of each crescent with a fork.

6 Lightly whisk the egg white and brush it over the biscuits (cookies). Dust with extra caster (superfine) sugar, if using.

7 Bake in a preheated oven, 200°C/400°F/ Gas Mark 6, for about 12-15 minutes. Leave the biscuits (cookies) to cool before serving.

COOK'S TIP

Store the citrus crescents in an airtight container or freeze them for up to 1 month.

Lemon Jumbles

Makes about 50

INGREDIENTS

100 g/3^1/2 oz/^{1}/3 cup butter, softened	1 egg, beaten	1 tsp baking powder
125 g/4^1/2 oz/^{1}/2 cup caster (superfine) sugar	4 tbsp lemon juice	1 tbsp milk
grated rind of 1 lemon	350 g/12 oz/3 cups plain (all-purpose) flour	icing (confectioners') sugar, for dredging

1 Lightly grease several baking trays (cookie sheets).

2 Cream together the butter, caster sugar and lemon rind until pale and fluffy.

3 Add the beaten egg and lemon juice a little at a time, beating well after each addition.

4 Sieve (strain) the flour and baking powder into the creamed mixture and mix together. Add the milk, mixing to form a dough.

5 Turn the dough out on to a lightly floured work surface and divide into about 50 equal-sized pieces.

6 Roll each piece into a sausage shape with your hands and twist in the middle to make an 'S' shape.

7 Place on the prepared baking trays (cookie sheets) and bake in a preheated oven, 170°C/325°F/Gas Mark 3, for 15-20 minutes. Leave to cool completely on a wire rack. Dredge with icing (confectioners') sugar to serve.

VARIATION

If you prefer, shape the dough into other shapes – letters of the alphabet or geometric shapes – or just make into round biscuits (cookies).

Chocolate & Lemon Pinwheels

Makes about 40

INGREDIENTS

175 g/6 oz/$^3/_4$ cup butter, softened 300 g/10$^1/_2$ oz/1$^1/_3$ cups caster (superfine) sugar	1 egg, beaten 350 g/12 oz/3 cups plain (all-purpose) flour	25 g/1 oz dark chocolate, melted and cooled slightly grated rind of 1 lemon

1 Grease and flour several baking trays (cookie sheets).

2 In a large bowl, cream together the butter and sugar until light and fluffy.

3 Gradually add the beaten egg to the creamed mixture, beating well after each addition.

4 Sieve (strain) the flour into the creamed mixture and mix until a soft dough forms.

5 Transfer half of the dough to another bowl and beat in the cooled melted chocolate.

6 Stir the grated lemon rind into the other half of the plain dough.

7 On a lightly floured surface, roll out the 2 pieces of dough to form rectangles of the same size.

8 Lay the lemon dough on top of the chocolate dough. Roll up the dough tightly into a sausage shape, using a sheet of baking parchment to guide you. Leave the dough to chill in the refrigerator.

9 Cut the roll into about 40 slices, place them on the baking trays (cookie sheets) and bake in a preheated oven, 190°C/375°F/Gas Mark 5, for 10-12 minutes or until lightly golden. Transfer the pinwheels to a wire rack and leave to cool completely before serving.

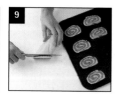

White Chocolate Cookies

Makes 24

INGREDIENTS

125 g/4^1/2 oz/^{1}/2 cup butter, softened
125 g/4^1/2 oz/^{3}/4 cup soft brown sugar
1 egg, beaten

200 g/7 oz/1^3/4 cups self-raising flour
pinch of salt

125 g/4^1/2 oz white chocolate, chopped roughly
50 g/1^3/4 oz brazil nuts, chopped

1 Lightly grease several baking trays (cookie sheets).

2 In a large bowl, cream together the butter and sugar until light and fluffy.

3 Gradually add the beaten egg, beating well after each addition.

4 Sieve (strain) the flour and salt into the creamed mixture and blend well.

5 Stir in the chocolate and brazil nuts.

6 Place heaped teaspoons of the mixture on to the prepared baking trays (cookie sheets). Do not put more than 6 teaspoons of the mixture on to each baking tray (cookie sheet) as the cookies will spread during cooking.

7 Bake in a preheated oven, 190°C/375°F/ Gas Mark 5, for about 10-12 minutes or until just golden brown.

8 Transfer the cookies to wire racks. Leave to cool before serving.

VARIATION

Use plain or milk chocolate instead of white chocolate, if you prefer.

Shortbread Fantails

Makes 8

INGREDIENTS

125 g/4^1/2 oz/^{1}/2 cup butter, softened
40 g/1^1/2 oz/8 tsp granulated sugar
25 g/1 oz/8 tsp icing (confectioners') sugar

225 g/8 oz/2 cups plain (all-purpose) flour
pinch of salt

2 tsp orange flower water
caster (superfine) sugar, for sprinkling

1 Lightly grease a 20 cm/8 inch shallow round cake tin (pan).

2 In a large mixing bowl, cream together the butter, the granulated sugar and the icing (confectioners') sugar until light and fluffy.

3 Sieve (strain) the flour and salt into the creamed mixture. Add the orange flower water, combine well and bring the mixture together to form a soft dough.

4 On a lightly floured surface, roll out the dough to a 20 cm/8 inch round and place in the tin (pan). Prick the dough well and score into 8 triangles with a round-bladed knife.

5 Bake in a preheated oven, 160°C/300°F/Gas Mark 2, for 30-35 minutes or until the biscuit (cookie) is pale golden and crisp.

6 Sprinkle with caster (superfine) sugar, then cut along the marked lines to make the fantails.

7 Leave the shortbread to cool before removing the pieces from the tin (pan). Store in an airtight container.

COOK'S TIP

For a crunchy addition, sprinkle 2 tablespoons of chopped mixed nuts over the top of the fantails before baking.

Millionaire's Shortbread

Makes 12 bars

INGREDIENTS

175 g/6 oz/1^1/$_2$ cups plain
(all-purpose) flour
125 g/4^1/$_2$ oz/^{1}/$_2$ cup butter,
cut into small pieces
50 g/1^3/$_4$ oz/3 tbsp soft brown
sugar, sieved (strained)

TOPPING:
50 g/1^3/$_4$ oz/10 tsp butter
50 g/1^3/$_4$ oz/3 tbsp soft brown
sugar

400 g/14 oz can condensed
milk
150 g/5^1/$_2$ oz milk chocolate

1 Grease a 23 cm/9 inch
square cake tin (pan).

2 Sieve (strain) the flour
into a mixing bowl and
rub in the butter with your
fingers until the mixture
resembles fine
breadcrumbs. Add the
sugar and mix to form a
firm dough.

3 Press the dough into
the prepared tin (pan)
and prick with a fork.

4 Bake in a preheated
oven, 190°C/375°F/

Gas Mark 5, for 20 minutes
until lightly golden. Leave
to cool in the tin (pan).

5 To make the topping,
place the butter, sugar
and condensed milk in a
non-stick saucepan and
cook over a gentle heat,
stirring constantly, until the
mixture comes to the boil.

6 Reduce the heat and
cook for 4-5 minutes
until the caramel is pale
golden and thick and is
coming away from the sides
of the pan. Pour the

topping over the
shortbread base and leave
to cool.

7 When the caramel
topping is firm, melt
the milk chocolate in a
heatproof bowl set over a
saucepan of simmering
water. Spread the melted
chocolate over the topping,
leave to set in a cool place,
then cut the shortbread
into squares or fingers
to serve.

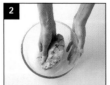

Vanilla Hearts

Makes about 16

INGREDIENTS

225 g/8 oz/2 cups plain (all-purpose) flour
150 g/5^1/2 oz/^{2}/3 cup butter, cut into small pieces

125 g/4^1/2 oz/^{1}/2 cup caster (superfine) sugar
1 tsp vanilla flavouring (extract)

caster (superfine) sugar, for dusting

1 Lightly grease a baking tray (cookie sheet).

2 Sieve (strain) the flour into a large mixing bowl and rub in the butter with your fingers until the mixture resembles fine breadcrumbs.

3 Stir in the caster (superfine) sugar and vanilla flavouring (extract) and bring the mixture together with your hands to make a firm dough.

4 On a lightly floured surface, roll out the dough to a thickness of 2.5 cm/1 inch. Stamp out 12 hearts with a heart-shaped biscuit cutter measuring about 5 cm/2 inches across and 2.5 cm/1 inch deep.

5 Arrange the hearts on the prepared baking tray (cookie sheet). Bake in a preheated oven, 180°C/350°F/Gas Mark 4, for 15-20 minutes until the hearts are a light golden colour.

6 Transfer the vanilla hearts to a wire rack and leave to cool. Dust with a little caster (superfine) sugar just before serving.

COOK'S TIP

Place a fresh vanilla pod in your caster (superfine) sugar and keep it in a storage jar for several weeks to give the sugar a delicious vanilla flavour.

2

3

4

Rock Drops

Makes 8

INGREDIENTS

200 g/7 oz/1³/4 cups plain (all-purpose) flour
2 tsp baking powder
100 g/3¹/2 oz/¹/3 cup butter, cut into small pieces
75 g/2³/4 oz/¹/3 cup demerara (brown crystal) sugar

100 g/3¹/2 oz/¹/2 cup sultanas (golden raisins)
25 g/1 oz/2 tbsp glacé (candied) cherries, chopped finely

1 egg, beaten
2 tbsp milk

1 Lightly grease a baking tray (cookie sheet).

2 Sieve (strain) the flour and baking powder into a mixing bowl. Rub in the butter with your fingers until the mixture resembles breadcrumbs.

3 Stir in the sugar, sultanas (golden raisins) and chopped glacé (candied) cherries.

4 Add the beaten egg and the milk to the mixture and bring together to form a soft dough.

5 Spoon 8 mounds of the mixture on to the baking tray (cookie sheet). Make sure they are spaced well apart as they will spread during cooking.

6 Bake in a preheated oven, 200°C/400°F/Gas Mark 6, for about 15-20 minutes until firm to the touch when pressed with a finger.

7 Remove the rock drops from the baking tray (cookie sheet). Either serve piping hot from the oven or transfer to a wire rack and leave to cool before serving.

COOK'S TIP

For convenience, prepare the dry ingredients in advance and just before cooking stir in the liquid.

Chocolate Chip Brownies

Makes 12

INGREDIENTS

150 g/5 1/2 oz dark chocolate,
    broken into pieces
225 g/8 oz/1 cup butter,
    softened
225 g/8 oz/2 cups self-raising
    flour

125 g/4 1/2 oz/1/2 cup caster
    (superfine) sugar
4 eggs, beaten
75 g/2 3/4 oz pistachio nuts,
    chopped

100 g/3 1/2 oz white chocolate,
    chopped roughly
icing (confectioners') sugar,
    for dusting

1 Lightly grease a
  23 cm/9 inch baking
tin (pan) and line with
greaseproof paper.

2 Melt the dark
  chocolate and butter in
a heatproof bowl set over a
saucepan of simmering
water. Leave to cool.

3 Sieve (strain) the flour
  into a separate mixing
bowl and stir in the caster
(superfine) sugar.

4 Stir the eggs into the
  melted chocolate

mixture, then pour this
mixture into the flour and
sugar mixture, beating well.
Stir in the pistachio nuts
and white chocolate, then
pour the mixture into the
tin (pan).

5 Bake in a preheated
  oven, 180°C/350°/Gas
Mark 4, for 30-35 minutes
until firm to the touch.
Leave to cool in the tin
(pan) for 20 minutes, then
turn out on to a wire rack.

6 Dust the brownie with
  icing (confectioners')

sugar and cut into 12 pieces
when cold.

COOK'S TIP

*The brownie won't be
completely firm in the
middle when it is removed
from the oven, but it will set
when it has cooled.*

Chocolate Macaroons

Makes 18

INGREDIENTS

75 g/2³/4 oz dark chocolate,
   broken into pieces
2 egg whites
pinch of salt

200 g/7 oz/1 cup caster
   (superfine) sugar
125 g/4¹/2 oz/1¹/4 cups
   ground almonds

desiccated (shredded) coconut,
   for sprinkling (optional)

1 Grease 2 baking trays (cookie sheets) and line with baking parchment or rice paper.

2 Melt the dark chocolate in a small heatproof bowl set over a saucepan of simmering water. Leave to cool slightly.

3 In a mixing bowl, whisk the egg whites with the salt until they form soft peaks.

4 Gradually whisk the caster (superfine) sugar into the egg whites, then fold in the almonds and cooled melted chocolate.

5 Place heaped teaspoonfuls of the mixture spaced well apart on the prepared baking trays (cookie sheets) and spread into circles about 6 cm/2½ inches across. Sprinkle with desiccated (shredded) coconut, if using.

6 Bake in a preheated oven, 150°C/300°F/Gas Mark 2, for about 25 minutes or until firm to the touch.

7 Leave to cool before carefully lifting from the baking trays (cookie sheets). Transfer to a wire rack and leave to cool completely before serving.

COOK'S TIP

Store the macaroons in an airtight container and eat within 1 week.

Florentines

Makes 8–10

INGREDIENTS

50 g/1³/4 oz/ 10 tsp butter
50 g/1³/4 oz/¹/4 cup caster (superfine) sugar
25 g/1 oz/¹/4 cup plain (all-purpose) flour, sieved (strained)

50 g/1³/4 oz/¹/3 cup almonds, chopped
50 g/1³/4 oz/¹/3 cup chopped mixed peel
25 g/1 oz/¹/4 cup raisins, chopped

25 g/1 oz/2 tbsp glacé (candied) cherries, chopped
finely grated rind of ¹/2 lemon
125 g/4¹/2 oz dark chocolate, melted

1 Line 2 large baking trays (cookie sheets) with baking parchment.

2 Heat the butter and caster (superfine) sugar in a small saucepan until the butter has just melted and the sugar dissolved. Remove the pan from the heat.

3 Stir in the flour and mix well. Stir in the chopped almonds, mixed peel, raisins, cherries and lemon rind. Place teaspoonfuls of the mixture well apart on the baking trays (cookie sheets).

4 Bake in a preheated oven, 180°C/350°F/Gas Mark 4, for 10 minutes or until lightly golden.

5 As soon as the florentines are removed from the oven, press the edges into neat shapes while still on the baking trays (cookie sheets), using a biscuit (cookie) cutter. Leave to cool on the baking trays (cookie sheets) until firm, then transfer to a wire rack to cool completely.

6 Spread the melted chocolate over the smooth side of each florentine. As the chocolate begins to set, mark wavy lines in it with a fork. Leave the florentines until set, chocolate side up.

This is a Parragon Book
First published in 1999
Parragon
Queen Street House
4 Queen Street
Bath BA1 1HE, UK

ISBN: 0-75253-358-4

Printed in China

Note
Cup measurements in this book are for American cups. Tablespoons are assumed to be
15 ml. Unless otherwise stated, milk is assumed to be full fat, eggs are medium and pepper
is freshly ground black pepper.